THE WORLD BOOK

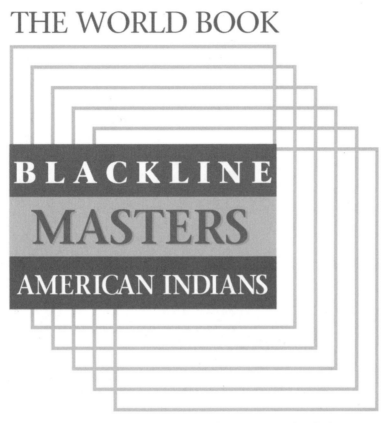

**BLACKLINE
MASTERS
AMERICAN INDIANS**

TERRITORIES AND WAYS OF LIFE

Editorial:	Shawn Brennan, Maureen Liebenson
Cartography:	Wayne Pichler
Art and Design:	John Horvath, Wilma Stevens
Production:	Kathe Ellefsen, Madelyn Underwood
Proofreading:	Anne Dillon, Chad Rubel
Manufacturing:	Marco Morales

World Book wishes to thank Ray Gonyea, Curator of Native American
Art and Culture, Eiteljorg Museum, Indianapolis, for his contribution to
The World Book Blackline Masters American Indians: Territories and Ways of Life.

For information on other World Book products,
call 1-800-WORLDBK (967-5325), or visit our
Web site at **http://www.worldbook.com**.

World Book, Inc.
233 N. Michigan Ave.
Chicago, IL 60601

ISBN 0-7166-7406-8

Printed in the United States of America
1 2 3 4 5 6 7 8 9 06 05 04 03 02 01

Table of Contents

American Indians

Introduction

The American Indians were the first people to live in the Americas. They were living there thousands of years before the Europeans arrived. Today, many Indians call themselves Native Americans. In Canada, they are called Aboriginal or native peoples.

The Indians probably came from Asia at least 15,000 years ago. At that time, there was a land area instead of water between Asia and North America. The Indians followed the animals they hunted across this "land bridge" from Asia to what is now Alaska. The distance was about 50 miles (80 kilometers). Today, the land that connected the continents is covered by water. It is called the Bering Strait.

Over time, the Indians spread all across the Americas. When Christopher Columbus arrived in 1492, Indians were living from the Arctic in the north all the way to the tip of South America. Columbus thought he had reached the Indies, which then included India, China, the East Indies, and Japan. So he called the people he met "Indians."

The Indians formed hundreds of groups, or tribes, across North and South America. Each tribe had their own way of life and their own language.

Although we call all these people American Indians, they were—and still are—very different from one another. This book will show how by highlighting the ways of life of the spectrum of Indian groups.

This book divides American Indians into 15 groups by area. Each group's section includes 2-6 pages of maps and scenes for your students to color. Some of these sections also include crafts and activities. There are also word searches, a crossword puzzle, and a matching game to test your students' knowledge and retention of the material in the book, and to sharpen their spelling of some of the names of important Indian tribes.

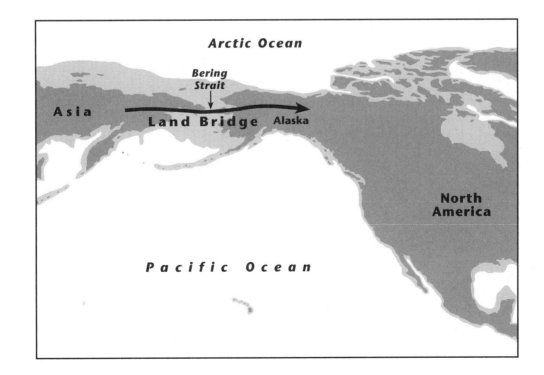

North and Central America

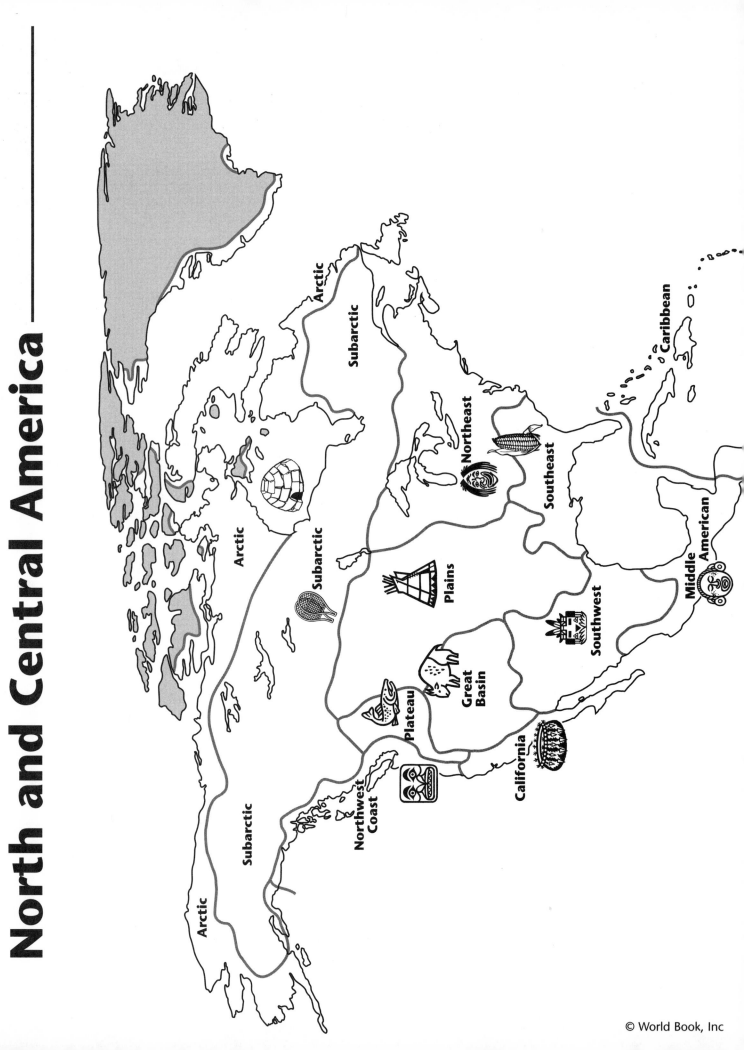

Arctic

Subarctic

Arctic

Subarctic

Subarctic

Caribbean

Northeast

Southeast

Plains

Southwest

Middle American

Great Basin

Plateau

California

Northwest Coast

Arctic

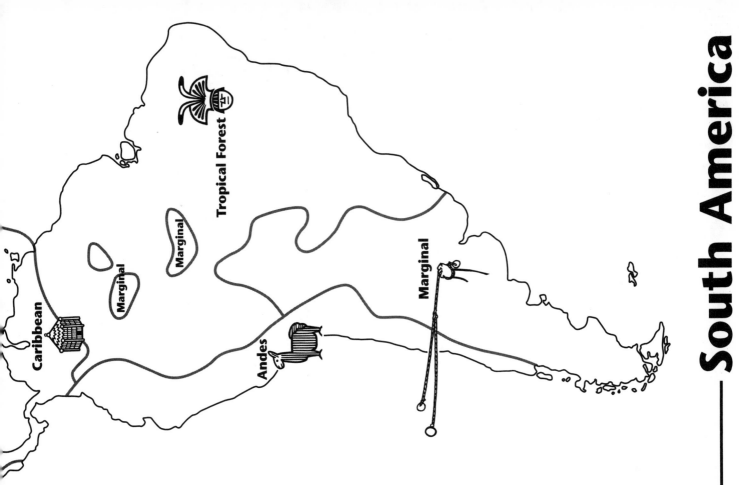

South America

Caribbean

Marginal

Marginal

Tropical Forest

Andes

Marginal

Arctic Region

Major Groups:

Aivilik Inuit
Aleut
Baffinland Inuit
Bering Strait Yuit
Caribou Inuit
Copper Inuit
East Greenland Inuit
Iglulik Inuit
Labrador Inuit
Mackenzie Inuit
Netsilik Inuit
North Alaskan Inuit
Pacific Yuit
Polar Inuit
Southwest Alaskan Yuit
West Greenland Inuit

North America

The people of the Arctic live farther north than any other people in the world. In North America, the Arctic includes most of the seacoast of Greenland, northern Canada, and Alaska (the areas shown in black on the map). The land consists mainly of tundra. In the winter, ice and snow cover the ground, and most of the Arctic Ocean is covered with ice.

Arctic Region

Inuit

An Inuk man prepares to go hunting. The Inuit and other Arctic peoples obtained food mainly by hunting and fishing. The Inuit lived in sealskin tents during the summer.

Arctic Region

Inuit

The Mackenzie Inuit wore caribou-skin parkas, trousers, and sealskin boots. The man is holding a harpoon, used for hunting whales, walruses, and other sea mammals. The Inuit used heavy wooden-framed sleds called sledges for transportation and hunting. The woman is holding a birchbark basket, used to store food. During the winter some Inuit built snowhouses called *igluliks*.

Arctic Region

Inuit Goggles Craft

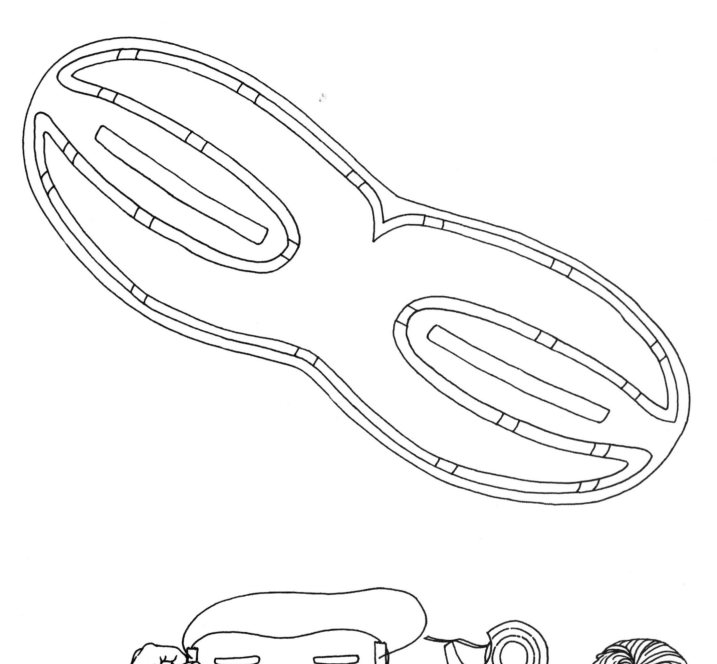

The Inuit often wore goggles of carved wood, bone, or ivory to reduce glare from the sun. The goggles had small holes or narrow slits through which to see. You can make your own goggles. Color the goggles on this page, cut them out, and fasten a piece of string or elastic to the back with tape to wear around your head. Don't forget to cut out the eye slits so you can see!

Subarctic Region

Major Groups:
Beaver
Carrier
Chilcotin
Chipewyan
Chippewa (Northern Ojibwa)
Cree
Dogrib
Han
Hare
Ingalik
Kaska
Koyukon
Kutchin
Montagnais
Naskapi
Sarcee
Sekani
Slavey
Tanaina
Tutchone
Yellowknife

North America

The Subarctic is a large semiarctic region that includes the interior of Alaska and most of Canada (the areas shown in black on the map). It is a land of cold winters and heavy snows. The Subarctic has many lakes and streams, and forests of fir, pine, spruce, and other evergreen trees.

12

Subarctic Region

Naskapi

During the cold Quebec winters, the Naskapi wore caribou skins painted with bright designs. They also wore short, round snowshoes which made it easy to trek through mountains. Men iced down their runners to make their sled glide across the snow and ice. The Naskapi lived in tepees made of caribou hide. The women smoke-tanned the caribou hides.

Subarctic Region

Chippewa

Chippewa women made clothes from animal skin. They put the skin over a log and scraped off the hair and fat with a sharp stone. The skin was then stretched tight on a frame and scraped again to make it smooth and soft. The women also cut and peeled poles to make wigwam frames and covered them with birchbark sheets.

Chippewa Headband Craft

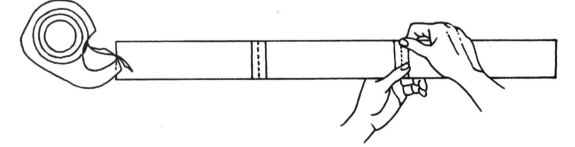

The Chippewa wore headbands decorated with woven feathers in designs like those on this page. You can make your own Chippewa-design headband. Color and cut out the three strips above. Tape two ends of the strips together, then measure to fit your head. Overlap or cut off the extra length. Then tape those two ends together to fasten around your head and wear. Try making your own designs on other strips too.

Northeast Region

North America

Major Groups:

Abenaki
Algonquin
Beothuk
Chippewa (Obijwa)
Delaware (Lenape):
   Munsee
   Unalachtigo
   Unami
Erie
Fox (Mesquakie)
Huron
Illinois
Iroquois:
   Cayuga
   Mohawk
   Oneida
   Onondaga
   Seneca

Kickapoo
Mahican
Maliseet
Massachusett
Menominee
Miami
Micmac
Mohegan
Nanticoke
Narragansett
Neutral
Ottawa
Pequot
Potawatomi
Powhatan
Sauk
Shawnee
Susquehannock
Tuscarora
Wampanoag
Winnebago

The Northeast culture area extends from just north of the Canadian border to just south of the Ohio River. It stretches from the Atlantic Ocean, including the coasts of Virginia and northern North Carolina, to about the Mississippi River. (The Northeast region is shown in black on the map). The Northeast has cold winters and warm summers. Forests cover much of the area, which is often called the Eastern Woodlands. Rolling prairies lie to the west.

Northeast Region

Menominee

Spearfishing was one way of catching fish. Menominee Indians used torches to lure the fish to the surface. Fish were an important source of food in the Northeast.

Powhatan

Pocahontas was the daughter of Powhatan, a famous Powhatan chief. She helped Indians and the early English settlers get along with one another. Captain John Smith, the leader of the settlers at Jamestown, Virginia, said that Pocahontas saved his life. Pocahontas is holding a type of basket made by Indians of the Northeast area.

Northeast Region

Mohawk (Iroquois)

The Mohawk performed war dances before raiding villages. Men held clubs as they danced around a wooden post. The leader struck the post with a hatchet. Mohawk and other Iroquois lived in 100-foot (30-meter) long houses made of poles covered with elm bark. There were separate sections for related families.

Northeast Region

Mohawk (Iroquois)

The Mohawk believed that certain kinds of sickness were caused by spirits, and could be cured only by spirits. So when Mohawk men and women got sick, they often sent for the False Faces to come and help them get well. The False Faces were men who belonged to a special club or society. The masks they wore represented the faces of powerful spirits that could cure diseases.

These wooden masks were carved from wood and painted. A mask carved in the morning was painted red. A mask carved in the afternoon was painted black. If the carving took both morning and afternoon, the mask was painted red and black. Strips of twisted bark were attached to the masks to look like hair.

Northeast Region

Mohawk Game

The Mohawk and other Iroquois played a game they called "the dish." This game was played with six wild plum seeds ground down smooth and flat on each side. They painted the seeds black on one side and white on the other. To play the game, three or four people made a "pot" of 100 dried beans. The plum seeds were placed in a wooden bowl. Each player took turns shaking the bowl and throwing the seeds into the air so that they turned over several times. If the seeds came down so that three or four were black or white, the player passed the seeds and bowl to the next player. If five seeds were all one color, the player took two beans from the pot. If all six seeds were the same color, the player took 20 beans. The player also took another turn if he or she won any beans. When all the beans were gone from the pot, the player with the most beans won.

You can play this Mohawk game, too. Instead of wild plum seeds, use six buttons. Paint or mark the buttons so that one side is different from the other. For the pot, use beans, as the Mohawks did, or other small things.

Southeast Region

North America

Major Groups:

Ais
Alabama
Apalachee
Atakapa
Caddo
Calusa
Catawba
Cherokee
Chickasaw
Chitimacha
Choctaw
Coushatta
Creek
Hitchiti
Lumbee
Natchez
Seminole
Timucua
Tunica
Yamasee
Yazoo
Yuchi

The Southeast extends from just south of the Ohio River to the Gulf of Mexico and from the Atlantic Coast of southern North Carolina to just west of the Mississippi River (the areas shown in black on the map). It is a region of mild winters and warm, humid summers. The terrain varies from the mountains of the Appalachians to the sandy coastal plain, with rolling hills and some swamps in between. Pine forests cover most of the region.

Southeast Region

Creek

After the Europeans arrived, Creek Indians wore clothes made of European cloth that they obtained through trade. They decorated their garments with a variety of beads, belts, and other ornaments. The Creek lived in palisaded, or fenced, towns. Each included a circular winter council house made of wood and bark and plastered with clay, with a thatched roof.

Southeast Region

Cherokee

The Cherokee played the game now called lacrosse. It was played with a small ball made of deerskin and stuffed with hair or moss. The players had two short sticks. Each stick had a net on the end. Players used the sticks to try to take the ball to the goal.

Southeast Region

Cherokee

Cherokee women made flour from corn kernels and sunflower seeds. They put the dried kernels or seeds into a hollow log. Then they crushed them by pounding them with a long, carved pole. Cherokee families lived in houses made of cane plant stems woven around poles stuck in the ground and covered with wet clay. The roof was made of chestnut tree bark. Families grew corn and other food plants in their garden.

Southeast Region

Cherokee

Sequoyah was a Cherokee Indian who invented a way of writing the Cherokee language. In 1821, he invented a set of 86 symbols that stood for the sounds used in speaking Cherokee. The Cherokee people learned Sequoyah's system quickly and used it to write books and newspapers in their own language.

Southeast Region

Cherokee Writing Activity

English	Cherokee	Pronunciation
sparrow	ᏥᏍᏆᏯ	chee ss KWAH yah
bird	ᏥᏍᏆ	chee ss KWAH
butterfly	ᎧᎹᎹ	kah MAH mah
deer	ᎠᏫ	kah WEE
I, *or* myself	ᎠᏯ	ah YAH
people	ᎠᏂ	ah NEE
wolf	ᏩᏯ	wah YAH

Here are some words as they are written with Sequoyah's symbols, and as they are spoken in Cherokee. Copy the symbols on flashcards with the Cherokee pronunciation and the English word on the back of the card. Test your Cherokee word skills by yourself or with a friend.

Plains Region

Major Groups:

Arapaho
Arikara
Assiniboine
Blackfoot:
      Blood
Piegan:
      Siksika (North Blackfoot)
Cheyenne
Comanche
Crow
Gros Ventre
Hidatsa
Iowa
Kansa
Kiowa
Kiowa-Apache
Mandan
Missouri
Omaha
Osage
Oto
Pawnee
Ponca
Quapaw
Sioux:
      Santee
      Teton
      Yankton
Tonkawa
Wichita

North America

The Plains stretch from just west of the Mississippi River to the Rocky Mountains and from Canada to Mexico (the areas shown in black on the map). Few Indians lived in this vast grassland region before the arrival of the Europeans. But after the Spaniards brought the horse to the region in the 1600's, a new way of life appeared on the Plains. On horseback, the Indians could follow the great herds of buffalo. After new tribes and white settlers arrived on the Plains, fighting broke out.

Plains Region

Sioux

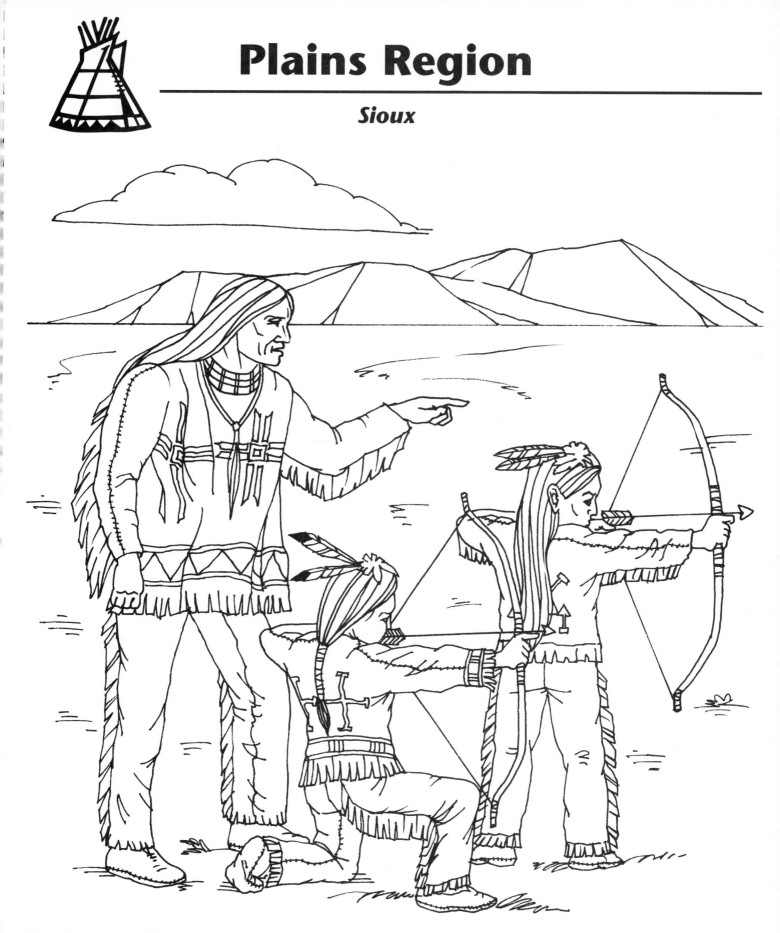

Sioux boys learned how to use small bows and arrows by practicing on still targets first and then on moving animals, such as jack rabbits. The early Plains Indians wore clothing made of deerskin.

Plains Region

Blackfoot

The most important and favorite food of the Blackfoot was buffalo. Before they hunted on horseback, Blackfoot men would wear the skin of a wolf to hunt buffalo. The buffalo weren't afraid of wolves, so they paid no attention to the disguised hunters. The men could creep up close and kill a buffalo with arrows.

Plains Region

Blackfoot

Curly Bear, a Blackfoot chief, lived more than 80 years ago. In this picture, Curly Bear is wearing the "dress-up" clothes that wealthy Plains Indians wore for special occasions.

Plains Region

Blackfoot Sign Language Activity

The Indian tribes of the Plains did not all speak the same language. But these people often had to communicate with one another. So the Blackfoot and other tribes worked out a sign language to talk to each other. Some of the signs used by the Plains Indians are shown on these two pages. The arrows indicate the direction of hand movements. Try to talk to a friend using Blackfoot sign language.

Father: Touch the right side of your chest several times with your right fist.

Mother: Touch the left side of your chest several times with your right fist.

I: Point to yourself with your right thumb.

You: Point to person with your right thumb.

Father   I

Hungry   Dog   Sleep   Drink

Thank you: Hold your hands chest high, palms facing out. Push your hands slowly toward the person you wish to thank, letting your hands curve downward.

Bird: Hold your hands at your shoulders, as shown. Move your hands up and down, like the flapping of a bird's wings.

Thank you   Bird

Arrow

Trade

Friend

Buffalo

Horse

Tepee

Indian

White man

Peace

Northwest Coast Region

Major Groups:
Bella Bella
Bella Coola
Chinook
Coast Salish:
    Chehallis
    Nisqually
    Puyallup
    Quinault
Eyak
Haida
Kwakiutl
Nootka
Quileute
Tillamook
Tlingit
Tsimshian

North America

The Northwest Coast stretches along the Pacific Ocean from southern Alaska to northern California (the areas shown in black on the map). Fish and seafood are plentiful in the ocean and the rivers of the region. Thick forests rise sharply from the beaches and include giant redwoods, Douglas fir, and pine trees. The region has a mild, humid climate.

Northwest Coast Region

Tlingit

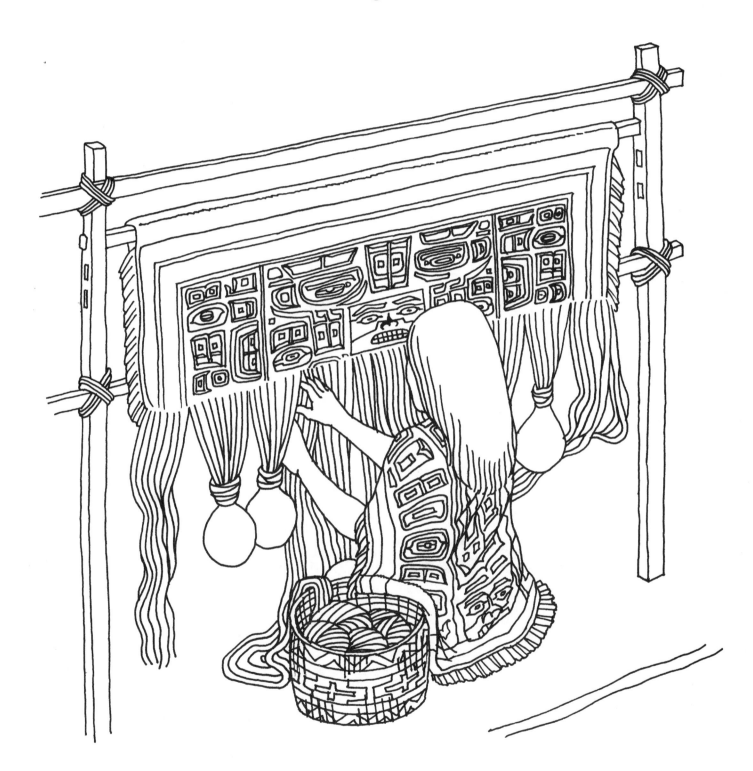

Tlingit women wove beautiful blankets from mountain goat wool and cedar bark. As they worked, the women followed patterns painted on boards that they kept beside them.

Northwest Coast Region

Tlingit

The thick forests of the Northwest Coast region provided wood for the Tlingit to build plank houses, canoes, and totem poles. Many of the men were skilled woodcarvers. A Tlingit chief rode in a canoe paddled by family or clan members. A man in a bear costume danced in the front of the canoe.

Northwest Coast Region

Haida

Northwest Coast Indians like the Haida built their villages near a lake, stream, or the sea where they had a plentiful supply of fish. The Haida were also skilled woodcarvers and carved totem poles with family emblems to show who lived in each plank house.

Northwest Coast Region

Totem Pole Craft

In the villages of Northwest Coast Indians, there were tall totem poles carved from tree trunks. Totem poles stood in the front of homes and in other public places and showed social rank and ancestry of a family or person. Carved on the poles were great grinning and frowning figures, one above the other. These are often shown as animals, because every chief believed that a magic animal had started his family, or helped or even married some of his ancestors. On these pages are some of the animals often seen on totem poles.

You can make your own "totem pole," too. Color the large design on the next page and cut it out. Then, on other pieces of paper, draw some of the designs from this page to make more totem heads, or design your own. After you have completed several totem heads, cut them out and tape them one above the other to a wall.

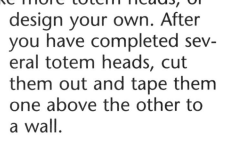

Thunderbird

Raven

Eagle

Hawk

Beaver

California Region

Major Groups:
Achumawi
Atsugewi
Cahuilla
Chumash
Costanoan
Hupa
Ipai
Karok
Luiseño
Maidu
Miwok
Monache
Pomo
Shasta
Tipai
Wappo
Wintun
Yana
Yokuts
Yurok

North America

The California culture area includes much of California. The area extends from the southern edges of Oregon in the north to Baja, in Mexico, in the south. It stretches from the Sierra Nevada in the east to the Pacific Ocean in the west. (The California region is shown in black on the map.) The landscape of the region varies from the northern redwood forests to the southern deserts. The climate is generally mild.

California Region

Pomo

Pomo women wove some of the most beautiful baskets in the world. They used the baskets to cook in and to keep things in. The women made a pudding by mixing acorn dough with water to make a paste. The paste was then put into a basket. The women cooked the paste by dropping hot stones, heated in a fire, into the basket.

Great Basin Region

North America

Major Groups:
Bannock
Gosiute
Kawaiisu
Paiute
Shoshone
Ute
Washoe

The Great Basin includes Nevada and Utah and parts of Oregon, Idaho, Montana, Wyoming, Colorado, New Mexico, Arizona, and California (the areas shown in black on the map). Much of the area is desert, with scattered grasses and sagebrush. Pine forests rise in the mountains and along streams and lakes. Summers are hot. In the northern part of the Great Basin and in the mountains, winters can be cold.

Great Basin Region

Shoshone

Shoshone Indians roasted pine nuts—the most important single source of food for Great Basin Indians—and made tea from wild plants. The Shoshone formed small family groups and moved from place to place in search of seeds, roots, fish, birds, and small animals such as rabbits.

Great Basin Region

Shoshone

Sacagawea (1787?-1812) was a Shoshone woman who helped guide explorers
Meriwether Lewis and William Clark through the Northwestern United States. She
helped the Shoshone and the explorers talk with one another.

Great Basin Region

Ute

After the introduction of the horse, the Ute became buffalo hunters. The Ute traditionally made tepees of buffalo skins. Ute children were laced up in cradles made of elkskin.

Plateau Region

Major Groups:
Cayuse
Coeur d'Alene
Flathead (Salish)
Kalispel
Klamath
Kutenai
Lillooet
Modoc
Nez Perce
Nicola
Okanagan
Palouse
Sanpoil
Shuswap
Spokane
Thompson
Umatilla
Walla Walla
Wanapam
Yakima

North America

The Plateau covers most of the southern half of British Columbia east of the coastal mountains. It also includes parts of Washington, Oregon, Idaho, and Montana, as well as a small section of northern California. (The Plateau region is shown in black on the map.) Forests and grasslands cover most of the north. The south is semidesert.

Plateau Region

Salish

The Flathead were a tribe of the Interior Salish Indians. They believed a flat head was beautiful. A board was tied to the padded skull of a Salish baby for a year, permanently flattening the forehead. Flathead women could build an animal skin tepee in a few minutes. In the winter, Salish lived in warm, pit houses with a smoke hole in the dirt roof.

Plateau Region

Nez Perce

Nez Perce men and boys fished each spring for salmon. Some fished in shallow water with spears or nets. Others fished from platforms of rock or wood built out from the shore. Some caught fish in traps made of brushwood and poles. The Nez Perce were noted for their breeding of the Appaloosa horse with its distinctive spotted coat.

Plateau Region

Nez Perce

Chief Joseph (1840-1904?) was a Nez Perce chief who was famous for leading his people away from battle. When the United States government ordered Joseph's people to move from Oregon to a reservation in Idaho, a war broke out. Joseph led his people more than 1,000 miles toward Canada.

Southwest Region

Major Groups:

Apache:
  Chiricahua
  Cibecue
  Jicarilla
  Lipan
  Mescalero
  San Carlos
  Tonto
  White Mountain
Coahuiltecan
Cocopa
Havasupai
Jumano
Karankawa
Maricopa
Mayo
Mohave
Navajo
Tohono O'odham
Pima

Pueblo:
  Hopi
  Keresan
  North Tiwa
  South Tiwa
  Tano
  Tewa
  Towa
  Zuni
Quechan
Seri
Tarahumara
Tehueco
Tepecano
Tepehuan
Walapai
Yaqui
Yavapai

North America

The Southwest, a huge, dry region, includes Arizona, New Mexico, southern Utah, southern Colorado, and northern Mexico (the areas shown in black on the map). In the northern area of the Southwest, wind and water have formed steep-walled canyons, sandy areas, buttes, mesas, and other landforms. In the south, the mountains give way to flat, desert country. The Rio Grande and the Colorado, Gila, and Salt rivers cut through the Southwest region.

Southwest Region

Hopi

Hopi priests painted their bodies and danced with live snakes in their mouths as part of their annual rain ceremony. This special ceremony reminded the kachinas—great weather spirits who lived in the mountains to the west—that rain was needed. Hopi women made beautiful bowls and jars from clay dug in the desert.

Southwest Region

Apache

The Apache traveled in small bands in search of food. They were fierce fighters who often raided the Pueblo Indians. They hunted deer, pronghorns, and rabbits, and gathered cactus fruit, roots, piñon nuts, and other plants. They wore animal skin garments. The Apache did not have permanent houses; some lived in brush shelters and tepees.

Southwest Region

Apache

Geronimo (1829-1909) was a Chiricahua Apache Indian. Around 1877, the United States government moved Geronimo's people to a reservation in Arizona. Geronimo escaped several times. In 1882, he and other Apache set up hidden camps in the mountains and made many raids. U.S. troops forced them to surrender in 1883.

Southwest Region

Kachina Mask Craft

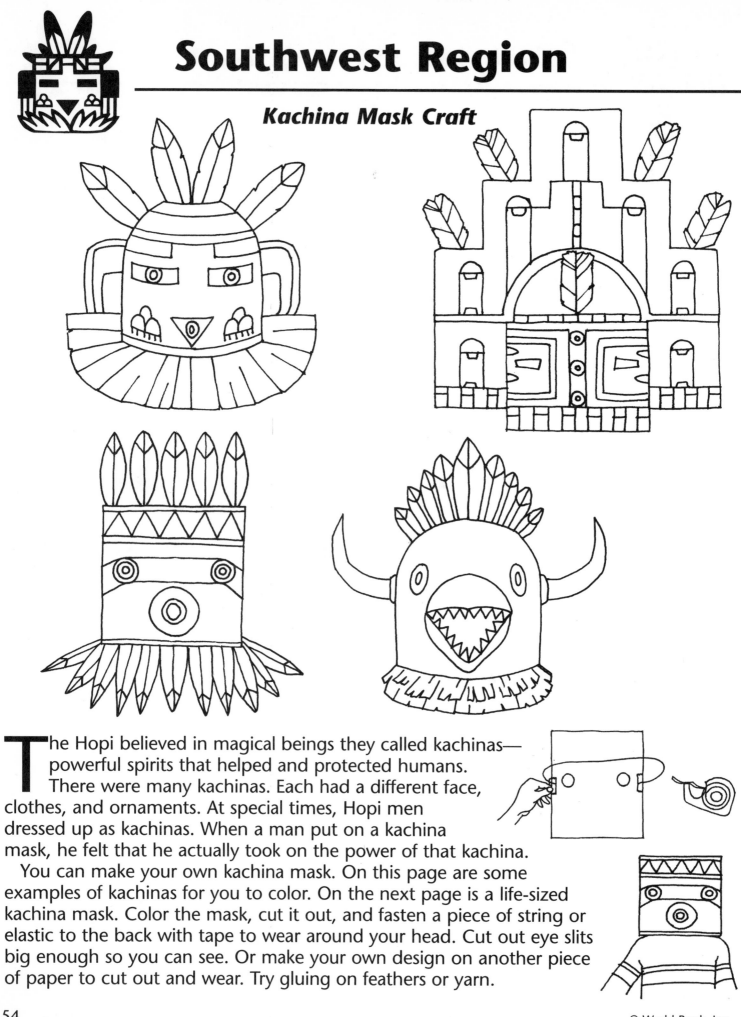

The Hopi believed in magical beings they called kachinas—powerful spirits that helped and protected humans. There were many kachinas. Each had a different face, clothes, and ornaments. At special times, Hopi men dressed up as kachinas. When a man put on a kachina mask, he felt that he actually took on the power of that kachina.

You can make your own kachina mask. On this page are some examples of kachinas for you to color. On the next page is a life-sized kachina mask. Color the mask, cut it out, and fasten a piece of string or elastic to the back with tape to wear around your head. Cut out eye slits big enough so you can see. Or make your own design on another piece of paper to cut out and wear. Try gluing on feathers or yarn.

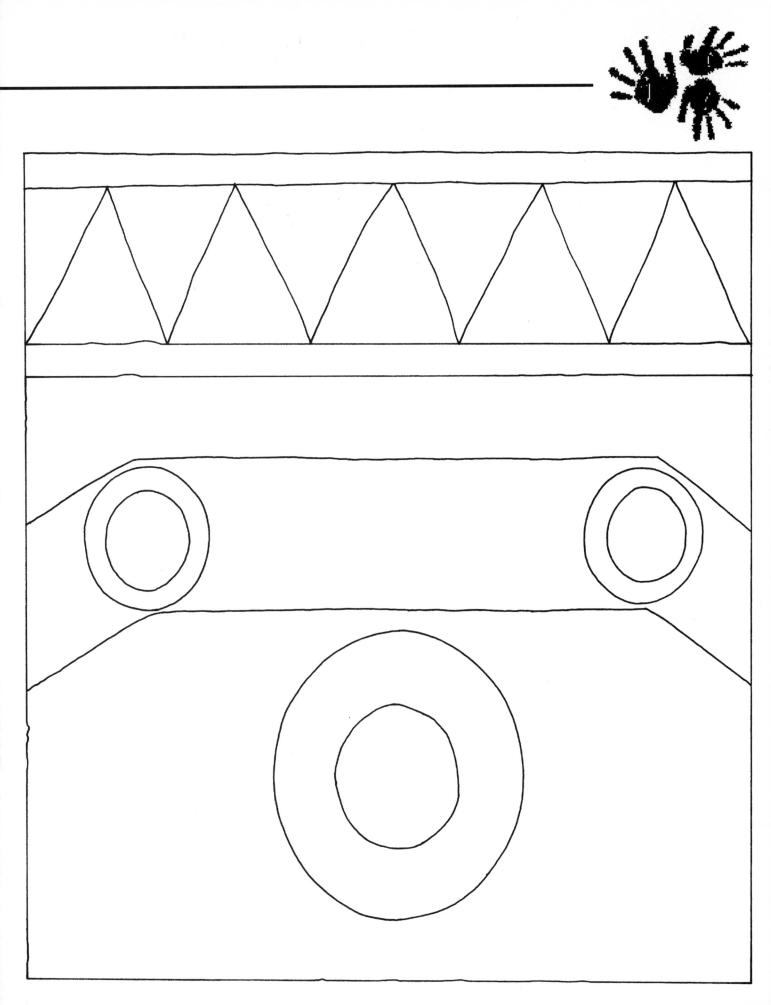

Middle America Region

Major Groups:

Aztec
Maya
Mixtec
Olmec
Otomí
Tarascan
Toltec
Totonac
Zapotec
Zoque

North America

South America

The Middle American Indians lived in what are now Mexico, Guatemala, and Honduras (the areas shown in black on the map). Part of the region lies in the tropics, but the altitude in the mountainous areas and on the plateaus of Mexico makes the weather comfortable the year around.

Middle American Region

Maya

The Maya built tall pyramids of limestone with small temples on top to worship their many gods. This Maya chieftain's daughter is holding a small figure of Yum Kax, god of the harvest. The Maya maiden is wearing an embroidered skirt fringed with jade beads, a headdress, and bracelets.

Middle American Region

Aztec

The Aztec had a great civilization. They had a kind of picture writing and knew how to work with numbers. Religion was very important to the Aztec. They built great temples and palaces and sacrificed prisoners to the Aztec gods. Jaguar Knights, soldiers who captured many prisoners, wore jaguars' heads over their own to show their bravery.

Middle American Region

Aztec

Quetzalcoatl (keht sahl koh AH t'l) was one of the most important gods to the Aztec. He was the god of life, civilization, the arts, and learning. The Aztec also believed he created the human race. He sometimes took the form of Ehécatl, god of the wind.

Caribbean Region

Major Groups:
Arawak
Carib
Chibcha
Chico
Ciboney
Cuna
Goajiro
Guaymi
Jirajara
Lenca
Lucayo
Miskito (Mosquito)
Motilones
Sub-Taíno
Taíno
Tairona

North America

South America

The Caribbean Indians lived throughout the southern half of Central America, the northern parts of what are now Colombia and Venezuela, and on the islands of the Caribbean Sea (the areas shown in black on the map). Although this region lies in the tropics, sea breezes or high altitudes make the climate pleasant throughout the year.

60

Caribbean Region

Carib

The Carib were a warlike group of South American tribes who lived
in small independent villages in the Amazon River Valley and the Guiana lowlands.
They hunted with traps, javelins, and clubs, and shot fish with poison arrows. Carib
boys had to prove their endurance and skill with weapons when they came of age. The
Carib wore clothes of cotton cloth, which they wove on looms.

Caribbean Region

Arawak

The Arawak were the first Indians that Christopher Columbus met in the Americas in 1492. The Arawak made canoes from hollowed-out logs that they used for fishing and to travel to other islands. The Arawak trained remoras to catch turtles. A remora is a large fish with a sticky patch on its head. The Arawak fastened a line to the fish. When the fish stuck itself to a turtle, both animals were pulled up.

Caribbean Region

Arawak

Arawak hunters built pens in which to catch animals called *hutias*. A hutia looks like a squirrel with a short, thin tail. The Arawak used dogs and torches to scare the hutias into the pens. The main kind of meat that the Arawak ate came from hutias.

Andes Region

Major Groups:
Araucanian
Atacama
Aymara
Barbacoa
Cañar
Cayapa
Chavín
Chimu
Colorado
Diaguita
Huari
Inca
Lipe
Nazca
Moche (Mochica)
Tarapaca
Tiwanaku (Tiahuanaco)
Uru

South America

The Andean Indians lived in the highlands of the Andes Mountains of South America and in nearby coastal areas. This large region includes southwestern Colombia, central Ecuador, coastal Peru, most of Chile, and parts of western Bolivia and Argentina. (The Andes region is shown in black on the map.)

Andes Region

Araucanian

Araucanian Indians are famous for their resistance to the Spaniards. They call themselves *mapuche,* which means "people of the country." They learned weaving from the Inca of Peru, who also tried to conquer them. Before that period, they wore guanaco-skin garments. Today, there are about 250,000 Araucanians.

Andes Region

Inca

Inca runners carried news and messages from all parts of the Inca empire. The runners traveled over roads and bridges built throughout the land. An Inca farmhouse had walls made of stones or clay bricks covered with clay plaster. The roof was made of dried, woven grass. The Inca raised llamas for carrying things and for food.

Andes Region

Inca

The Inca ruled a vast, rich empire. Most city buildings were planned and built by men we would now call architects. Using only stone hammers and bronze chisels, Inca builders were able to cut and smooth blocks and fit them together so well a pin couldn't be pushed between them. Many Inca buildings still stand. Inca nobles rode on frameworks called *litters*, which held couches and were carried on men's shoulders.

Andes Region

Inca Panpipe Craft

The Inca enjoyed music. They made one kind of musical instrument by fastening together several wooden tubes of different lengths. Blowing into each tube made a different note. We call this instrument a panpipe. You can make a pretend panpipe that's easy to play.

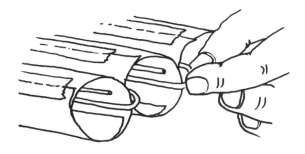

Color and cut out each of the three rectangles on the next page. Roll up each rectangle to make tubes of different lengths. Tape each tube closed.

Cover one end of each tube with a piece of wax paper held in place with a small rubber band. Use paper clips to fasten the tubes together at the open ends. The open ends should all line up. Stretch a large rubber band around all three tubes to hold them together. Punch a hole in the middle of each tube with a pencil.

To play your panpipes, hum loudly into the open ends of the tubes. Keep your mouth slightly open. When the holes in the tubes are open, the wax paper will buzz. Covering the holes changes the sound.

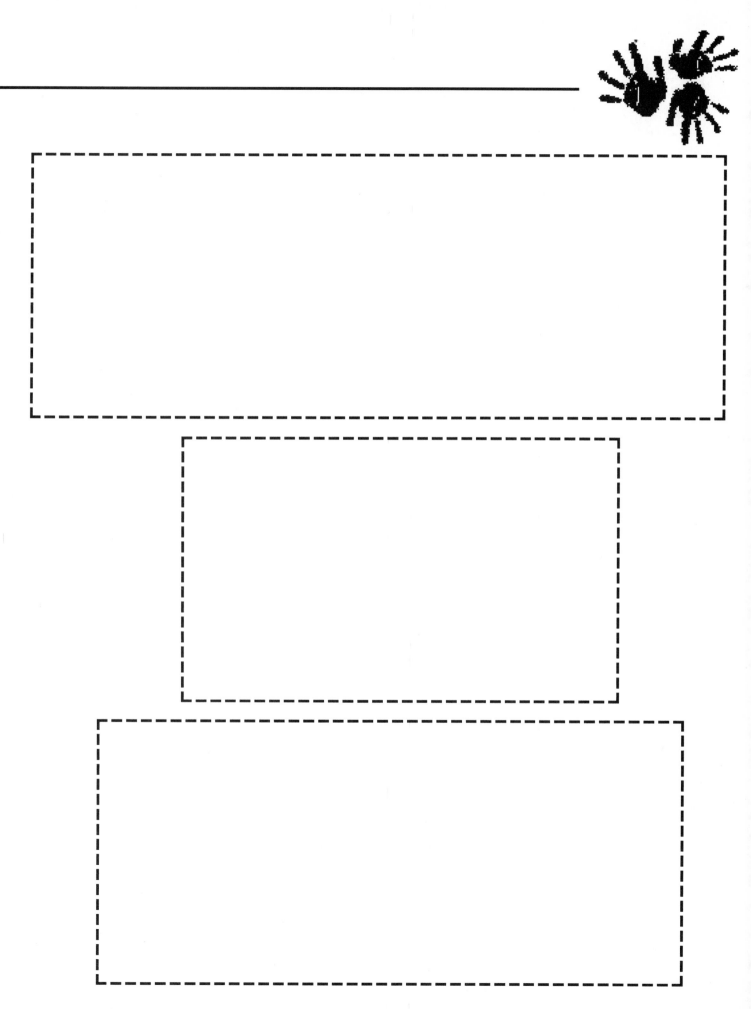

Tropical Forest Region

Major Groups:
Amahuaca
Arara
Arawak
Arua
Camacan
Campa
Carajá
Cariri
Conibo
Gé:
    Bororo
    Caingang
    Kayapó
    Sherente
    Timbira
Guaicuru
Guayaná
Jívaro
Kuikuru
Mojo
Pano
Taulipang
Tucuna
Tupi-Guaraní:
    Chiriguano
    Guaraní
    Mundurucú
    Omagua
    Sirionó
    Tupina
    Tupinamba
Witoto
Yagua
Yamamadi
Yanomami
Yawalapiti

South America

Indians of the Tropical Forest lived along rivers and in the jungles that cover almost all of what are now Guyana, Suriname, and French Guiana; much of Brazil; southern Colombia and Venezuela; and eastern Bolivia and Peru. (The Tropical Forest region is shown in black on the map.) Farming was the main source of food in this hot, humid region.

Tropical Forest Region

Yawalapiti

Yawalapiti men made special costumes and musical instruments that they used for religious ceremonies. They often wore strips of woven cotton on their arms and legs. Both men and women wore necklaces made of stone beads. They also decorated their bodies and hair with paint. Black paint was made by mixing charcoal with fat; red paint was made from berries.

South American Marginal Regions

Major Groups:
Abipón
Alacaluf
Ashluslay
Charrúa
Chono
Guató
Macú
Mataco
Mbayá
Mura
Nambicuara
Ona
Payaguá
Puelche
Querandi
Sirionó
Tehuelche
Yahgan
Zamuco

South America

Indians of the Marginal Regions barely managed to exist on the poor lands of eastern and southern South America (the areas shown in black on the map). Most of these Indians lived on the plains, which had little plant or animal life. Those who lived on the cold, rainy coasts also lacked natural resources.

South American Marginal Regions

Gauchos

Some Indians of the Marginal Regions became *gauchos* (cowboys) after the white people brought horses to the area. Indians of the South American plains hunted *guanacos*, animals related to camels that look like llamas, and *rheas*, birds that look like small ostriches, with *bolas*. Bolas were stone or clay balls attached to the ends of a rope.

Matching Game

Each of the symbols on the left-hand side of pages 74-75 represents an American Indian region. The pictures on the right-hand side of these pages are of people and activities you read about in each region. Match each of the symbols on the left to the picture that goes with it on the right by drawing a line from the symbol to the picture.

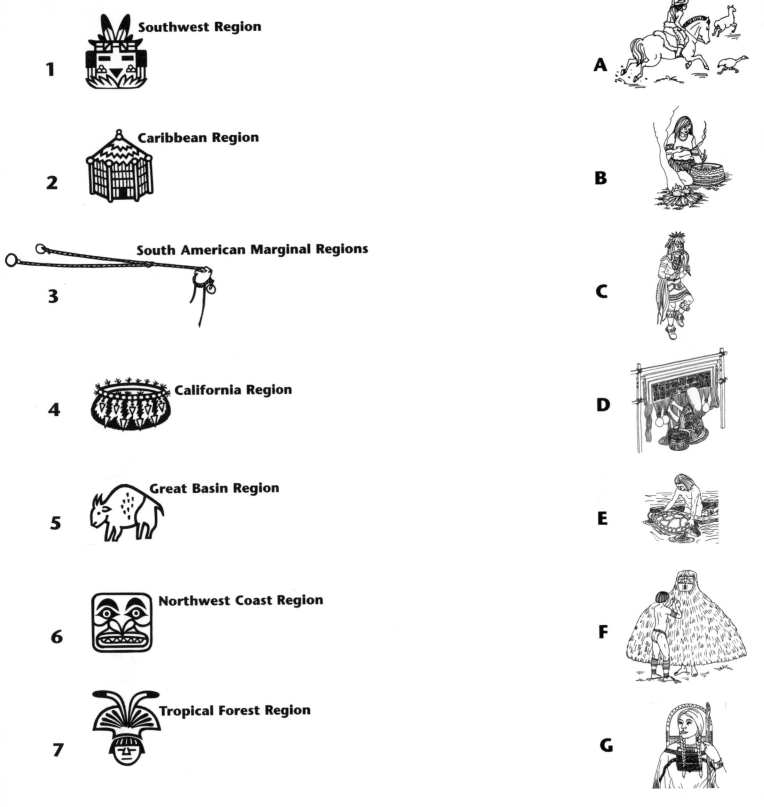

Southwest Region

1

Caribbean Region

2

South American Marginal Regions

3

California Region

4

Great Basin Region

5

Northwest Coast Region

6

Tropical Forest Region

7

A

B

C

D

E

F

G

8 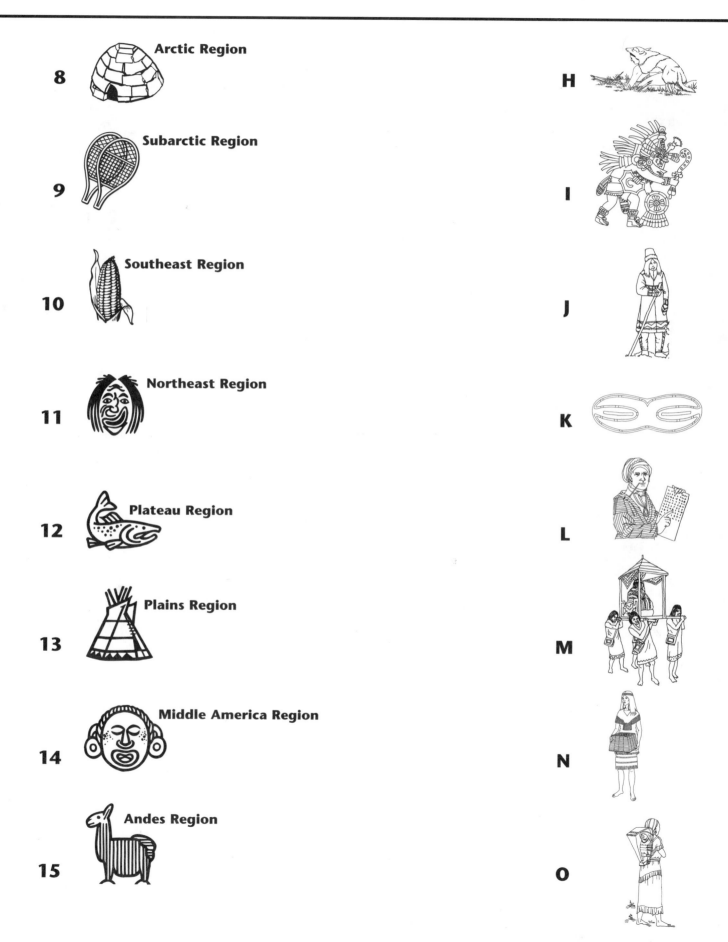 Arctic Region

H

9 Subarctic Region

I

10 Southeast Region

J

11 Northeast Region

K

12 Plateau Region

L

13 Plains Region

M

14 Middle America Region

N

15 Andes Region

O

Crossword Puzzle

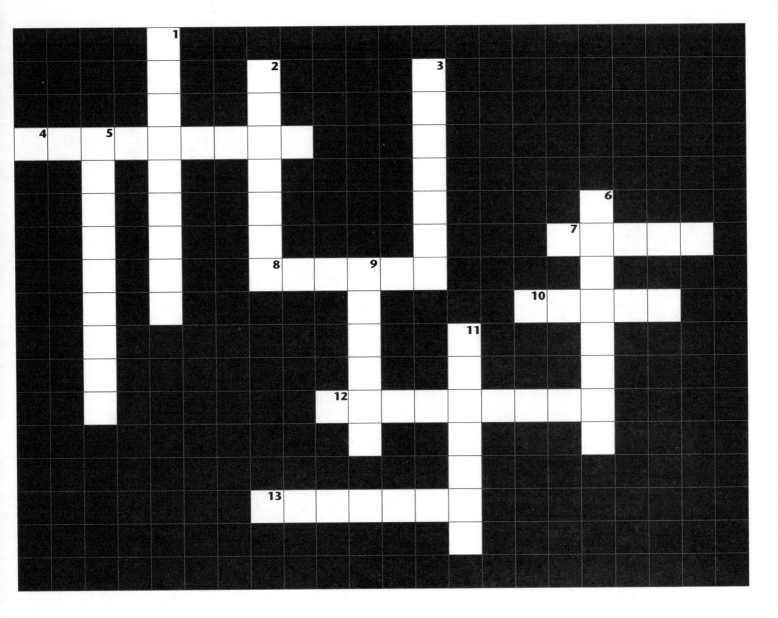

Across

4. The Mohawk and other Iroquois wore this wooden mask to represent powerful spirits.
7. This cone-shaped tent is made of bark, mats, or animal skin.
8. This is the first group of Indians Columbus met.
10. This Arctic group lives in northern Alaska, Canada, and Greenland.
12. This Shoshone woman helped guide Lewis and Clark through the Northwestern United States.
13. The Inca played this musical instrument.

Down

1. Northwest Coast Indians carve family and clan symbols on this tall wooden structure.
2. This brightly decorated Hopi doll or dancer represents a spirit.
3. The Inuit build this snowhouse.
5. This large, rectangular shelter was built by the Iroquois.
6. This Cherokee Indian invented a system for writing the Cherokee language.
9. This dome-shaped shelter is made of leaves or bark.
11. The Inuit wore these "glasses" to reduce the glare from the snow and sun.

Word Search

North and Central American Indians

Hidden in the letters below are the names of some important North and Central American Indian groups. Words may be hidden horizontally, vertically, or diagonally and may be forward or backward. One tribe is circled to get you started. Find and circle the rest.

```
K N S Q U W A A S B G N E Z P E R C E N F C A
P S H O S H O N E T E T E F F O J A V A N I T
R N M T I G N I L T G P F M R Y I L A Q E E P
Y H E G J K S Z O R Y M B O P W K E H O M J D
C Y K M W P D E N P A C F K T F L B O P B E U
O I T S U H H O I E B H Y N A W C O T W N Q P
M E I Z I S T O M U M E C V J P E R V U R T M
A P U H L I Y N E K U R E A F L A Y A M D E B
N D N H M L W G S T E O T E P R E F R I C I R
C K I E Y A A B A E W K Z T S A A B O K P R L
H S W P B S Y A W N B E A U O I E N I R S O I
E I O L O T H G O W S E P M P E V E H R T Q X
N O P R E Z A D P O I F O A W S Y S I A H U R
N J I E A J U E R A W I K F D A Z U R D O O D
E V T W K V I K N V D S A E K U A Y V I S I J
Y O E C H I P P E W A O S I O L V W S A J S N
E W I J Y I D N T N M P M Y I N A T A H W O P
H R K L O M S X U O I A C J S T U B D R F U A
C H O C T A W Z E R K O M O E E N I M O N E M
```

Aztec	Comanche	Menominee	Powhatan	Tlingit
Cherokee	Haida	Naskapi	Salish	Yakima
Cheyenne	Inuit	Navajo	Seminole	
Chippewa	Iroquois	Nez Perce	Shoshone	
Choctaw	Maya	Osage	Sioux	

Word Search

South American Indians

Hidden in the letters below are the names of some important South American Indian groups. Words may be hidden horizontally, vertically, or diagonally and may be forward or backward. One tribe is circled to get you started. Find and circle the rest.

```
A C K E Y O M O C H E E H C L E U H E T T
N I E T H E S B E T Z E R B L E U A O I A
K E N T A C Y O F L R A W P E N A L E W S
E E N A Z C A O X M Y R N E H J T S B A Y
L L O C V A T N I R A U H U S E F U F N O
E I R O P T W O K E M P O L T A R R Y A L
A S K N O I N K I R A C L E R N O N E K U
H A K E T J I H N A C N I K I N B S A U L
C A K O L Y E N E R A K J U L E I O P A C
I I T J C N U D O N T U S O E E R R T Y R
M O A U I N A L A W A R A R N K S A O B U
O N G L O I N I A A R N A B E Y A V T A Q
T E U I C G N N O T Y A N O M A M I L B U
O L C E H A R E M I I A I N I A O J I H A
N U K A C O R O N O S U G I N O N I L O P
K A Y U B I T I C H L I O U T I N I E S T
A R A V I L A U B H O L E N A E O J P S E
T R A C L R U T R E A J Y S E B R O F U R
A B K A C N E K S N I T I P A L A W A Y T
```

Araucanian	Huari	Nazca	Witoto
Atacama	Inca	Tehuelche	Yagua
Carib	Jivaro	Tiwanaku	Yanomami
Gê	Moche	Tupinamba	Yawalapiti

Answer Key

P. 74 Matching Game

1 - C	9 - J
2 - E	10 - L
3 - A	11 - N
4 - B	12 - O
5 - G	13 - H
6 - D	14 - I
7 - F	15 - M
8 - K	

P. 76 Crossword Puzzle

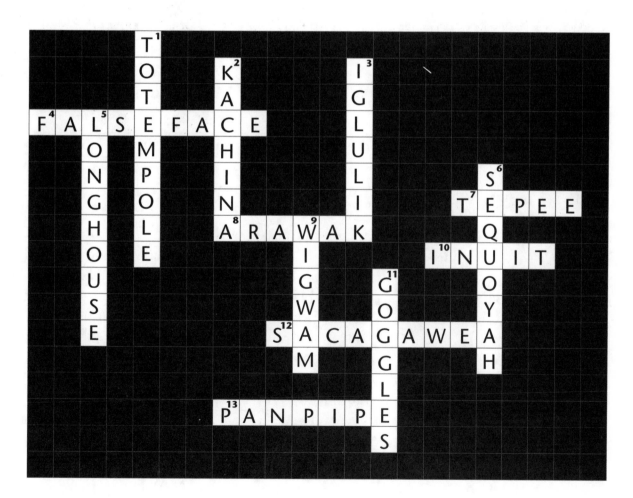

Answer Key

P. 77 Word Search: North and Central American Indians

```
K N S Q U W A A S B G N E Z P E R C E N F C A
P S H O S H O N E T E T E F F O J A V A N I T
R N M T I G N I L T G P F M R Y I L A Q E E P
Y H E G J K S Z O R Y M B O P W K E H O M J D
C Y K M W P D E N P A C F K T F L B O P B E U
O I T S U H H O I E B H Y N A W C O T W N Q P
M E I Z I S T O M U M E C V J P E R V U R T M
A P U H L I Y N E K U R E A F L A Y A M D E B
N D N H M L W G S T E O T E P R E F R I C I R
C K I E Y A A B A E W K Z T S A A B O K P R L
H S W P B S Y A W N B E A U O I E N I R S O I
E I O L O T H G O W S E P M P E V E H R T Q X
N O P R E Z A D P O I F O A W S Y S I A H U R
N J I E A J U E R A W I K F D A Z U R D O O D
E V T W K V I K N V D S A E K U A Y V I S I J
Y O E C H I P P E W A O S I O L V W S A J S N
E W I J Y I D N T N M P M Y I N A T A H W O P
H R K L O M S X U O I A C J S T U B D R F U A
C H O C T A W Z E R K O M O E E N I M O N E M
```

P. 78 Word Search: South American Indians

```
A C K E Y O M O C H E E H C L E U H E T T
N I E T H E S B E T Z E R B L E U A O I A S
K E N T A C Y O F L R A W P E N A L E W I S Y
E E N A Z C A O X M Y R N E H J T S B A N O L
L L O C V A T N I R A U H U S E F U F A K U L
E I R O P T W O K E M P O L T A R R Y A A C R
A S K N O I N K I R A C L E R N O N E A K U U
H A K E T J I H N A C N I K I N B S A U U Q
C A K O L Y E N E R A K J U L E I O P A Y C A
I I T J C N U D O N T U S O E E R R A V Y B R U
M O A U I N A L A W A R A R N K S A O T A B Q U
O N G L O I N I A A R N A B E Y A V A Q U A
T E U I C G N N O T Y A N O M A M I L B U A P
O L C E H A R E M I I A I N I A O J I H A S E
N U K A C O R O N O S U G I N O N I L O P T E
K A Y U B I T I C H L I O U T I N I E S T R
A R A V I L A U B H O L E N A E O J P S E
T R A C L R U T R E A J Y S E B R O F U R
A B K A C N E K S N I T I P A L A W A Y T
```